The Butterfly

Edited by Gillian Doherty
With thanks to Michael Crosse and the team
at the London Butterfly House for information about butterflies

The Butterfly

Anna Milbourne

Illustrated by Cathy Shimmen

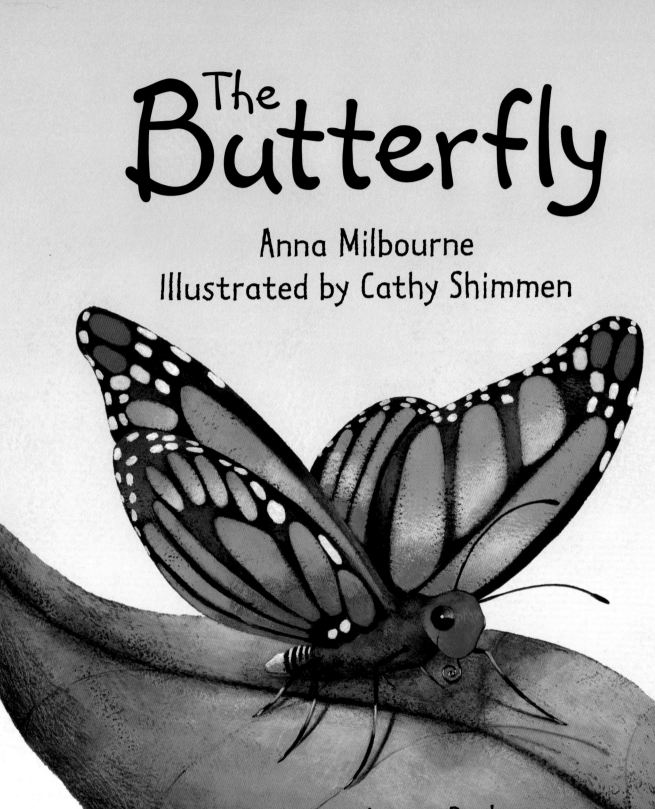

Designed by Laura Parker

At the end of the garden,
there's a little stripy caterpillar.

What do you think
it's been doing all day?

First, it ate up the leaf
it was sitting on.

And when that
was gone...

it started munching
on the next one.

There are lots of other hungry caterpillars too.

There's a teeny-tiny green one

a very chubby yellow one

a soft, white hairy one

and a big, fat
fuzzy one.

And all of them are eating as fast as they can chew.

The little stripy caterpillar is not so little now.

But **still** it keeps on eating...

munch

munch

munch

Soon it's even too fat for its skin.

So it shrugs it off, like it's just an old coat...

and then it eats
some more.

One day, the caterpillar stops eating.

Perhaps it's full.

It curls up under a leaf
and falls fast asleep.

Slowly, its skin becomes
a shiny case.

It hangs there quietly,
not moving at all...

for a very long time.

All at once it starts to wriggle.

It wriggles and wriggles
until the case splits open,
and it inches its way out.

The stripy caterpillar has become
a beautiful butterfly.

It stretches out its bright,
new wings in the warm sunshine.

Then it flutters up into the wide, blue sky.

All kinds of pretty butterflies
are flitting around the garden.

There's a lacy white one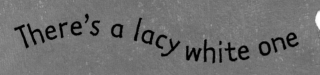

two speckled blue ones

and one with circles on its wings.

The butterfly flutters from flower to flower...

sipping sweet nectar
from every one.

At night, it folds
its dainty wings...

and settles down to sleep.

When it's time, the butterfly carefully lays some eggs.

Each one is like a tiny pearl.

A few days later...

a little stripy caterpillar
pops out of each egg.

They are all
very, **very** hungry.

Can you guess what happens next?

munch

munch

munch

munch